# FACT CAT

# BIRDS

Izzi Howell

**WAYLAND**

www.waylandbooks.co.uk

## FACT CAT

**Get your paws on this fantastic new mega-series from Wayland!**

Join our Fact Cat on a journey of fun learning about every subject under the sun!

First published in Great Britain in 2015 by Wayland
Copyright © Wayland 2015

MIX
Paper from responsible sources
FSC® C104740
www.fsc.org

Wayland
An imprint of Hachette Children's Group
Part of Hodder & Stoughton
Carmelite House
50 Victoria Embankment
London EC4Y 0DZ

An Hachette UK Company
www.hachette.co.uk
www.hachettechildrens.co.uk

A catalogue for this title is available from the British Library
Printed and bound in China

Produced for Wayland by
White-Thomson Publishing Ltd
www.wtpub.co.uk

Editor: Izzi Howell
Design: Clare Nicholas
Fact Cat illustrations: Shutterstock/Julien Troneur
Other illustrations: Stefan Chabluk
Consultant: Kate Ruttle

Picture and illustration credits:
Corbis: Tui De Roy/Minden Pictures 19; iStock: evil_ss 4tl, Guillermo Perales Gonzalez 4br, Jonathan Woodcock 7b, JK-photo 9, Kenneth Canning 13, Anoliso1 17t, KeithSzafranski 17b, Craig Dingle 20; Shutterstock: Donjiy cover, Ondrej Prosicky title page and 12, Jesse Nguyen 4tr, john michael evan potter 4br, Kateryna Larina 5, MagMac83 6, Paul Reeves Photography 7, Nagel Photography 8, Andrzej Kubik 10, duangnapa_b 11, Stephanie Periquet 14t, David Steele 14b, Sergey Ryzhov 15, Cheryl E. Davis 16, Wollertz 18, feathercollector 21.
Every effort has been made to clear copyright.
Should there be any inadvertent omission, please apply to the publisher for rectification.

The author, Izzi Howell, is a writer and editor specialising in children's educational publishing.

The consultant, Kate Ruttle, is a literacy expert and SENCO, and teaches in Suffolk.

## FACT CAT FACT

There is a question for you to answer on each spread in this book. You can check your answers on page 24.

# CONTENTS

# WHAT IS A BIRD?

Birds are a group of animals that are similar to each other in certain ways. Birds have wings and they are covered in feathers. Young birds (called chicks) hatch from eggs.

Lorikeets, cardinals, cranes and gulls are all different types of birds. Which country has the grey crowned crane as its national bird?

lorikeet

cardinal

grey crowned crane

yellow-legged gull

Birds are **warm-blooded** animals. This means that they can control the temperature of their bodies. In hot weather, birds lose heat by **panting** or by spreading out their wings.

The flamingo often stands on one leg, so that only one of its legs is in the cold water. This helps it to stay warm.

FACT CAT **FACT**

Flamingos are pink because they eat a lot of **algae**, which contain a natural pink **pigment**. If a flamingo stopped eating algae, its feathers would turn white!

# HABITAT

Birds live in different **habitats**, from rainforests and lakes to deserts and oceans. Some birds, such as parrots, live high in the branches of trees. Other birds, such as ostriches, never leave the ground.

Many birds, such as pigeons, live in towns and cities. Which name do we give to white pigeons?

Some birds, such as gulls, spend much of their time near water. However, almost all birds come on to land to lay their eggs and take care of their chicks.

Some birds, such as this barn swallow, **migrate** to warm habitats during the winter months. They return to colder habitats in spring to lay their eggs.

FACT CAT **FACT**

The Arctic tern travels over 80,000 kilometres every year, migrating from the Arctic to Antarctica and back again.

# BREATHING

nostril

All birds need to breathe air. When a bird breathes in, its **air sacs** and **lungs** take **oxygen** from the air and send it around their bodies.

The peacock, like most birds, can breathe through its mouth or its nostrils.

Having air sacs as well as lungs means that a bird can take in more oxygen from the air than other types of animal. This means that birds can fly high in the sky, where there is less oxygen than there is on the ground.

The common crane breathes through its air sacs and lungs to give it enough oxygen to fly at heights of up to 10,000 metres!

**FACT CAT FACT**

The kiwi is the only bird with nostrils at the end of its long **beak**. Most birds have nostrils on top of their beaks. Which country does the kiwi come from?

# WINGS

Birds use their wings to fly. When a bird pushes air down with its wings, it moves higher. Birds move forwards by pushing air backwards with their wings.

All birds have wings, but some birds, such as ostriches, can't fly. Can you find out the name of another bird that cannot fly?

## FACT CAT FACT

Instead of flying, ostriches use their long legs to run at speeds of up to 64 kilometres per hour!

Birds' wings are covered in soft feathers. This smooth **surface** helps birds to move their wings quickly through the air.

Birds twist the tips of their wings to change the direction they are flying in.

# DIET

Carnivorous birds, such as owls, have sharp beaks, which they use to hunt small animals and cut through meat. Herbivorous birds, such as cockatoos, pick fruit and nuts from trees with their beaks.

A hummingbird has a long thin beak that can reach deep into flowers to drink nectar.

FACT CAT FACT

The hummingbird is the only type of bird that can fly backwards! How did the hummingbird get its name?

This bald eagle has just caught a fish in its claws.

**Birds of prey**, such as eagles and hawks, use their sharp **claws** to help them hunt fish and small **mammals**. Once they have caught their **prey**, they carry it in their claws to a safe place where they can eat it.

# NESTS AND EGGS

Some **female** birds lay eggs in nests. They make nests from grass or branches. Other birds lay their eggs in underground **burrows** or in shallow holes in the ground.

Large groups of village weavers build nests that hang from the branches of the same tree. The nests are made from grass and dried leaves.

ostrich
egg

chicken
egg

Ostriches lay the
largest eggs of any
bird. Each ostrich egg
weighs the same as
20 chicken eggs!

Birds' eggs come in many
different sizes and colours.
Most birds lay more than one
egg at a time. One chick
will hatch from each egg.

FACT CAT FACT

It would take almost two hours to hard-
boil an ostrich egg! How long does it
take to **hard-boil** a chicken egg?

# YOUNG

Birds' eggs must be kept warm so female birds sit on their eggs until their chicks are ready to hatch. Each chick breaks out of its egg using a sharp part of its beak called an egg tooth.

FACT CAT FACT

The shell of a bird's egg looks thin, but it is very strong! This is so that the shell is not broken by the weight of the female bird.

After a few weeks, the eyes of these **newborn** robin chicks will open and their feathers will grow.

Female ducks take their chicks onto water to teach them how to find their own food. What is another name for a young duck?

After hatching from their eggs, most chicks stay in their nests until they have grown bigger. Their parents try to keep them safe from **predators**. Most birds bring their chicks food to eat.

The emperor penguin feeds its chicks with fish that it has carried back from the ocean in its stomach.

# SENSES

The most important **sense** for birds is sight so that they don't fly into other birds in the air. Carnivorous birds need to be able to see prey on the ground when they are high up in the air.

Like most birds, the aracari toucan has an eye on each side of its head. This means that it can see a wide area of land or sky at one time.

Hearing is also important for birds. They can recognise other birds by the sounds that they make. Chicks call for their parents when they are hungry or if they are in danger.

The barn owl hunts at night. It uses its sense of hearing to work out where small animals, such as mice, are hiding.

FACT CAT FACT

Some birds can learn to repeat words spoken by humans. One budgerigar could say over 1,700 different words! Can you find out the name of another type of bird that can learn to speak?

# STRANGE BIRDS

The cassowary is the most dangerous bird in the world to humans. If it feels scared, it will attack by kicking and cutting predators with the sharp claws on its feet.

The middle toe of a cassowary has a 10 centimetre-long claw! How many toes does a cassowary have on each foot?

claw

The wandering albatross spends most of its life flying above the ocean. Its wings are so large that it can **glide** in the wind for hours without flapping its wings once!

The **wingspan** of a wandering albatross can be up to 3.4 metres, which is more than the height of an adult man!

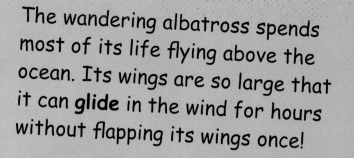

FACT CAT FACT

Albatrosses can live to be 60 years old. In their lifetime, they will travel millions of kilometres!

**Try to answer the questions below. Look back through the book to help you. Check your answers on page 24.**

**1** Young birds hatch from eggs. True or not true?

a) true

b) not true

**2** Which bird can't fly?

a) parrot

b) ostrich

c) pigeon

**3** Birds of prey are herbivores. True or not true?

a) true

b) not true

**4** Chickens lay the biggest eggs of any bird. True or not true?

a) true

b) not true

**5** What do emperor penguin chicks eat?

a) fish

b) nectar

c) insects

**6** When do barn owls hunt?

a) in the afternoon

b) in the morning

c) at night

# GLOSSARY

**air sac** a part of a bird's body that is used for breathing

**algae** a plant-like living thing that lives in water and doesn't have a stem or leaves

**beak** the hard outer part of a bird's mouth

**bird of prey** a large bird that kills smaller animals for food

**burrow** a hole in the ground dug by an animal to live or lay eggs in

**carnivorous** describes an animal that only eats meat

**claw** a sharp curved nail on the foot of an animal

**female** describes a bird that lays eggs from which chicks will hatch

**glide** to move through the air without using wing power

**habitat** the area where a plant or an animal lives

**hard-boil** to cook an egg until the inside is solid

**herbivorous** describes an animal that only eats plants

**lung** a part of the body that is used for breathing

**mammal** a type of animal with fur that gives birth to live young

**migrate** to travel from one place to another at the same time each year

**nectar** a sweet liquid made by plants that is found inside flowers

**newborn** describes something that has just been born

**oxygen** a gas in the air that animals need to breathe to live

**pant** to breathe with the mouth open and the tongue out

**pigment** something that gives something else its colour

**predator** an animal that kills and eats other animals

**prey** an animal that is killed and eaten by other animals

**sense** an ability that helps us to understand the world, such as sight, hearing, touch, smell and taste

**surface** the top part of something

**warm-blooded** describes an animal that can keep its body temperature the same regardless of its surroundings

**wingspan** the distance between the ends of a bird's wings

# INDEX

# ANSWERS

## Pages 4–21

**Page 4:** Uganda

**Page 6:** Dove

**Page 9:** New Zealand

**Page 10:** Some flightless birds include penguins, emus and cassowaries.

**Page 12:** From the humming sound made by its flapping wings.

**Page 15:** Around 10-12 minutes

**Page 17:** Duckling

**Page 19:** Some birds include parrots, lyrebirds and mockingbirds.

**Page 20:** Three

## Quiz answers

1   true

2   b - ostrich

3   not true – they are carnivores.

4   not true – ostriches lay the biggest eggs of any birds.

5   a - fish

6   c - at night

# OTHER TITLES IN THE FACT CAT SERIES...

## Space
The Earth 978 0 7502 8220 8
The Moon 978 0 7502 8221 5
The Planets 978 0 7502 8222 2
The Sun 978 0 7502 8223 9

## United Kingdom
England 978 0 7502 8927 6
Northern Ireland 978 0 7502 8942 9
Scotland 978 0 7502 8928 3
Wales 978 0 7502 8943 6

## Countries
Brazil 978 0 7502 8213 0
France 978 0 7502 8212 3
Ghana 978 0 7502 8215 4
Italy 978 0 7502 8214 7

## History
Neil Armstrong 978 0 7502 9040 1
Amelia Earhart 978 0 7502 9034 0
Christopher Columbus 978 0 7502 9031 9
The Wright Brothers 978 0 7502 9037 1

## Habitats
Ocean 978 0 7502 8218 5
Rainforest 978 0 7502 8219 2
Seashore 978 0 7502 8216 1
Woodland 978 0 7502 8217 8

## Geography
Continents 978 0 7502 9025 8
The Equator 978 0 7502 9019 7
The Poles 978 0 7502 9022 7
Seas and Oceans 978 0 7502 9028 9

## Early Britons
Anglo-Saxons 978 0 7502 9579 6
Roman Britain 978 0 7502 9582 6
Stone Age to Iron Age 978 0 7502 9580 2
Vikings 978 0 7502 9581 9

WAYLAND
www.waylandbooks.co.uk